THE RADIANCE OF PIGS

BOOKS BY STAN RICE

THE RADIANCE
OF PIGS

Poems by
STAN RICE

ALFRED A. KNOPF
New York, 1999

THIS IS A BORZOI BOOK
PUBLISHED BY ALFRED A. KNOPF, INC.

Copyright © 1999 by Stan Rice

All rights reserved under International and Pan-American Copyright Conventions.
Published in the United States by Alfred A. Knopf, Inc., New York, and simultaneously
in Canada by Random House of Canada Limited, Toronto. Distributed by Random
House, Inc., New York.

www.randomhouse.com

Knopf, Borzoi Books, and the colophon are registered trademarks of Random House, Inc.

Library of Congress Cataloging-in-Publication Data
Rice, Stan.
    The radiance of pigs : poems / by Stan Rice. — 1st ed.
      p.   cm.
    ISBN 0-375-40485-6 (alk. paper)
    I. Title
PS3568.I295R33 1999   98-43232
811'.54—dc21   CIP

Manufactured in the United States of America
First Edition

§ CONTENTS

I CHILDHOOD

II HADES

CONTENTS

III   *RESURRECTION*

I CHILDHOOD

I remember Paris
Texas, where my great-uncle owned a glass factory,
Whose bedroom was mirrors, even the doors,
Who had a white cat that slept on the towels
In the bathroom cabinet, named Whiteboy,
And it was there I met my first genius,
My great-aunt's brother, a dwarf,
Who sat in a dwarf rockingchair
On the front porch, rocking.
Nearby were Palestine, Moscow, Athens.

The rabbit I ran
Until I caught
Throbbed in my hand
The whole thing a heart.
Had frozen, to vanish, to turn weed-grey.
I brought it home
And put it in my yard
And brought them to see
What I'd caught was gone.
Stupid to think a rabbit would stay.

Common sparrow, city sparrow,
Brown, grey, black, plump, narrow,
Barely visible, by the millions,
Less noticed even than pigeons,
I have no place for you,
I study your anonymous (even ugly)
Plenitude, it's like
Loving life for no reason,
The ordinary, the vacant lot,
The individual leaves,
The millionth father pretending
To throw his gleefully squealing
Son into the Mississippi.

§ WHEN I GROW UP

Wm Yeats claimed when he was old
He wanted to be hammered gold.
Even if you throw in Gift Of Prophecy
That's a dumb fate; even for artifice,
Which is eternal and all.
Not that I want to be a salmon
Turning hook-nosed and scarlet
As I rot in fertilized roe. Nor would
I want to be a roasted golden brown turkey.
I want to be mercury.

The snowmen go to sea
In manly little boats.
The wind balloons the sails.
The snowmen float

From emerald island to emerald island
With neither dread nor grief.
They drink hot chocolate
In shade of sails

And in the starlight sleep.
Starlight, oakum, creaking timber.
And on the storm the smell of mint.
Some are seasick

Others tender.
They bend to heave the bow about,
And their corncob pipes fall out,
And their carrot noses

Ride the swells,
And their coal eyes fall through coral.
Yet still they sail
Without fear or sorrow.

Then the calm. Their sails
Deflate. They laugh like carrion.
Their jaws cave in.
They wet the decks.

A little tragedy is knowledge
And knowledge of none is comic.
The snowmen know there is no craft
To reconstruct their crystal vomit

Nor fallen faceparts into masks,
Yet go to sea, to die on water,
Instead of on lawns as rotted clowns
In black top hats.

§ ANTS

The acid ants, the acidic ants, flowering
On the piece of melon in the saucer,
Making milky the wedge of cheese,
Are a garnet, burst into pieces of life,
On the pale pale saucer.
I hold the magnifying glass over them
And stare down as through a hole of water.
They shred with their ice tong jaws, shred and hurry,
Their antennae touch and touch, their
Black rears become more swollen,
They have exoskeletons, spikes,
They take the sweetness back to the queen
For she alone lays the eggs
With the eyeballs like goldfish in condoms.

§ GARDEN

When I had a garden
The radishes would harden under the dirt
Until I pulled them.
I was amazed!
I gave them to my mother, who would throw them away.
I didnt mind. I knew she would.
What are radishes
Good for but growing.
And also what amazed me was
That the carrots
Got so orange
In the dark, in the dirt.
She threw them away too.
Now that did hurt.

§ THE BRAVE

I was rehearsing how I would
Be brave at the inevitable
Death of Father and finding
Myself mostly a coward.

The horrible part
Was that I enjoyed
Thinking it through.
I am really trying
Next time not to be so impatient with the dying.

§ DONT PUT HIM IN THE FREEZER

Dont put him in the freezer.
He loathes being there.
The pain-chair is his preference.
Which is a paradox, I know.
Dont put him on the butcherpaper either
Even if he has a fever
That makes him shake like a golden retriever
Just out of water. In truth
If I were the doctor I would
Bring a wheelbarrow to work,
So without a lot of bother
I would constantly know where I had put
The illuminated and diapered Father.

Dad is dead,
So in the family portrait Im painting he wont cast
A shadow on the seaside grass.
And because Ive fitted his 70 year old head
On his 32 year old body his neck will looked stretched.
His tie will be black,
And his suit grey,
And he'll stay that way.
I think I may go away, too.
Weary of being dumb
To the sensual beauty of place
I am beginning to prefer
The transcendence of flaying.
I mean some huge risk, that will skin my body
And put what is left on a pole
In a painting.
Not where Dad went.
Who said one thing about that:
"So, in a poem, a word can mean more than one thing."
Which meant he'd read my book.
I want to be a greek god, or rather
A mortal who having been bronzed
By the flames of psychological pain
Is made a god on paper. Or
Maybe a radio cowboy with nothing but
A great voice and an implied horse.
Not what Dad got.

Stay busy, Mother, you
White butterfly,
Whose only friend,
The brown butterfly, is dead.
For you will not find
In all the greenery one such as him.
Find some flowers to fly among
That remind you of his companionship.
Bring him the pollen
And nectar with the butterfly's
Great power.
Stay busy, loving the gathering,
That when his ghost mounts you
You may turn tan with his shadow.

Why is it that my father
Seems the same dead as alive?

My friend,
Who thought himself
Inferior to me—
Child of the man,
My childlike father—

Relaxed again.

At noon the black carriage horse
Cocks its rear leg
At the "ankle." The people
Search for
The King of the Dead.

From post to post I go,
My shoulders low,
My senses
Interior.
My head I have plucked
From a vine in the bible
And placed on the
Fishscale roof of the building.
Watchman!

A thread of melody
Can lead to a granary
In Hades.
And in that granary
An angel
Masturbates with a lighted candle.
Her aphrodisiac is being lonely.
The grain gives way
With a whisper.
She is naked
But for humanskin sandals.
Her toenails are fishscales.

When she climaxes
The candle flares up;
Rain runs down windows;
The pine tree
Feels all its needles.

And there
In the orange roar
Is father, mowing.

§ FIRST AND THEN

First there is the grief.
Then the relief
That his pain is over.
Then that your pain is over.
Then the guilt
At your relief.
Then that grief.

I am Anger, a poisonous
Frog, blood-splashed butter,
Do Not Come Near.
I am sincere. And who is she?
She is my wife, Fear.
She frightens me. I want to be near
Her. I sit on her breast and pulse
And puff up my cheeks of skin.
Then I jump into her brown eye.
It begins to cry.
Now what have I done
Again.

§ LUST

Lift your skirt.
I want to see you.
And the oleaginous
Guilt and drink
Flushed from the cut fruit.
Bend over with your shoes on.
Your hair falls forward.
Your breasts
Are pulled by the mass of the earth.
Now lie down.
I want your anklet
To sparkle on your calf.
The whites of your eyes
To be above your pupils.
Without shame
Fill the mirror
Until it oozes
For lust has left me
And I need you to make me
Fear no more
The small black pig in the peach.

§ *EARLY SPRING*

Silver lipstick is
On the japanese plum
Leaves. We are in our second stage of love.
After flesh falters, after
The eyes we knew look at us
As a stranger.
It's early spring again.
Nature's voluptuous skeleton
Sits up!

§ KEEPER

Keeper, keep out
The wrongs, the angers.
Keep them in a manger.
Let Adam and Eve sleep
Spoonstyle by a brainless river.
Keep them from danger.
Here come the men on stilts!
Let them in.
They talk of craft with angels.
And keep my wife and me
From the life of wrongs and angers.
Keep us as amazed as we were the night
The cradle blazed.
Bluer, slower, deeper,
Keeper.

Anne is in Rio
And Im in New York.
The first New Years Eve
In thirty-four years we have not
Been together.
I have left the mini-blinds down
So that when I move my head
The streetlights of Queens
Tremble like stars.
I have never done that before.
Anne on the Amazon. No
Streetlights on the black East River.
I sleep with the pillow between my legs,
The breastless pillow.

Sheba, believe me, she
With her brains in her panties
Could not lure me
From your crackling smile
And brown eyes, though she
Straddle my chest for a nickel,
Though she pay *me,* those things
Are fleeting, they age, they change
Like the adorable puppy
Into the coffeetable of hair.

Yes, Sheba, that other,
That naked neck with the gold hair
Gathered up in a clip,
Below which slopes skin
To breasts as firm
As the bellies of infants,
And that head which would fall back
And breathe in if I kissed them,
And gods rush through the holes
In the lace—but what then?
I would grope for the one
Who knows all my faults
And find an idiot.

Estrangement from Sheba
Makes me make songs,
As the Jews did in the psalms
Crying out for their God
To re-love them. When Sheba
Fears me, and calls me brute,
When I am to her the hairy heart
Making the shoebox move,
I sing—of our youth,
When being a monster was ok,
So long as he checked the gasjets and locks.
Pity him, Sheba, for the beast
He is is the beast you loved.

O my Sheba,
Solomonize me. Shake from my cornucopia
The chopped off hands and heads
Of my enemies. Empty me. Take
In your little hands the TV remote. I give it you.
And set the thermostat wherever you want it,
Forever.
Or at least until it gets too hot in this room for you too.

She sleeps all night, all day.
There is no other way.
She cannot see. The sun is black,
The food is tasteless,
The landscape waste.
And though she sleeps she does not dream.
It seems unfair to go so deep
And see no more than when awake.
It is unfair. But that's the deal.
This is why we call it change.
It usually does.
We suffer this we suffer that.
Then one day sleep seems not the thing.
And we wake up and things are not
Discrete, discrete.
But every paradox resolves. The oak
The sky the nest the crown
The crows the kings. She wakes up
And sees in Seeing
All her fears as feasting forms.
And writes it down.
And there you go.
A book of changes.

I had to go to Hades
Because I wanted a dark beer.
Anne stayed above, drinking
The golden stuff. Once there
I couldnt get enough.
The other inhabitants were going through hell
So they didnt know I was constantly drunk.
I stayed there about ten years
And grew more and more charming.
I was constantly hung-over, of course,
But it was a price I was willing to pay
For being considered such a nice person.
Eventually I got so tired of being sick in the mornings
I quit; and immediately surfaced.
For two years I was ok.
My colleagues even elected me chairman.
Then one day one of them treated me
As if I were Satan; and then another.
They thought I wanted power.
All I wanted was to be desired.
But I was sober, and so moved on.
Being drunk is like being dead,
And a death to fear.
But there's one other thing I'd like to make clear.
In Hades they brew a great dark beer.

§ I OPEN THE WINDOW

I open the window when it rains.
The red sable paintbrushes still in their brown paper bags
Feel no pain.
When the ivy-covered telephone poles
On Airline Highway
Are full of snails
The prostitutes come out.
We do not know how low
The heart can go before
It cannot hold anymore
Red foam.
Under the orange motel neon
Their milky skin
In fishnet hose.
Dont tell me so-and-so
Is waiting in Heaven.
They are not even waiting in Oakland.

I am only looking for things
I cannot fathom.
Nothing else is worth looking for, or at, or into,
Unless it is bottomless,
Shivering with itself,
Like the Bottomless Lake
In Carlsbad Caverns, black as oil,
Pierced slightly by the flashlights
Of the guides, with only a rope
Between me and it, and because of this
I am cursed with ten thousand angers
And the small vision
Of what's wrong with things.

§ BLOODRIGHT

That was what gave the parade in
Florence preceding the brutal football
Game its authenticity. These horsemen
Were not elected burghers but were
Directly descended from the families
That ruled by bloodright from when
Savonarola and the Medicis were
Murdering each other for power.
They had not been chosen by some
Democratic process to represent
Their districts in a costume show,
But sat in their saddles in slashed
Ballooned tri-colored trousers and
Blouses as those who could even now,
Given a little anarchy, with lifted chins
And expressions of bored power canter
Down cobblestones with their enemies
Heads on poles.

§ THE PUNISHMENT

Will I be punished for having no psychology at all to speak of
But only two cueball eyes and a penchant for vividness;
Will I be punished for having written "Ignore Thyself"
In a reversal of the Socratic dictum
And then having done so assiduously for years
Until I could only sit on the TV couch
Watching pornography and boxing;
Will my vanity and lack of empathy haunt
My old age as my obsession with sensual pleasure
Haunted my youth; will I be punished
For my constant presumption of innocence
Even though I can see my guilt clearly
In the way I walk when I walk past the hidden
Video camera monitor in Sears? Yes
I will be. By you,
Beautiful.

§ *LONG LIFE*

The phallus enters dry,
And exits shining,
And enters shining.

I always thought importance would not be my fate,
That I would be, like my father, a plumber of poetry,
Under the house, with the black widows, melting a pot of solder.

Everyone
I learn late
Is specific
And no affection
Begun in amazement
Wasted.

I go to the Civil Sheriff
To get a permit to carry a gun.
What have I done?
Ive bought a Walther .380,
Which is what Q insisted James Bond
Carry. It's flat. It feels ok
Against the small of my back.
I know somebody who knows somebody
Who knows about stalkers.
We have one.
He was arrested on a train in Denver
For threatening women. He told the psychiatrist
He was headed to kill my wife.
His train ticket destination was New Orleans.
He was returned to California to serve more time
For breaking parole then moved straight from San Quentin
To across the river.
He rang our doorbell at 7 a.m., a
Sunday. Living like this is No Fun.
I go to the Civil Sheriff's office
To get a permit to carry a gun.
Im worn out on theories.
Im sure you have one.

Drunkenness said,
"I will give you certainty
But kill you early."
So I chose the long life of not knowing.

§ DAY AFTER BAD DREAM

Flagstones shining in sunlight,
After rain, after the bad dream, please
Be my god, Guide,
Through violence
And cowardly Time.
Make me grasp its nylon jacket
So the hood squashes its beard.
Make its left hook stop like a blur in a photo
When it realizes I did not intentionally
Trample its foot.
Our eyes fixed inches apart
In a moment of anger and pride. Please,
After pride and anger, let there be closure.
Guide this, my only self,
Through a rage at injustice
That might turn violent, and cost me art,
My day job.

§ STALLION

The rapist horse,
I saw him in a field,
His glistening pink penis
Almost as long as his leg,
Just asking for it.
This sight was more
Than some of my companions
Wanted to see. I understood.
But as for me I felt like
I had for the first time
Seen why the Greek gods
Had been believed in by
Such otherwise rational men.

A black cat
Studded with raindrops
Stopped on the lawn.
Cats dont shake dry
Like a dog. Not this
Cat, this day. Froze,
And hissed,
"What I have missed I have missed,"
And slunk off.
Afterwards, how will we feel?
After the great risk that was wrong.

I have closed my eyes
And thought too much.
As penalty I will
Never be able to relax.
Rope will wrap the bone.
Marble-dust will clam the palm.
The stuffed roosters will have glass eyes.
But I wont be able to sleep or wake up.
My poems will make no sense.
Soda will crust my edge.
I'll look down from the height of my head.
No one else will uncover
The nakedness of the leg of lamb.
Normal conversation will drive me mad.
My coat will collapse.
Anxiety will be proof of life.
To have lived will be proof of the photograph.
In the places of torture
The unimaginable will remain unimagined,

Until the words pull down ⎰ their wet red masks.
⎱ their tight white pants.

§ MEETING SATAN IN THE PARKING LOT

Last night a dog followed me to my car
In the parking lot of the restaurant and I thought
Satan has come.
First he made seductive ringing of metal like bells,
Which were his tags.
All over him was his black beard.
His eyes were very clear amber for a dog,
And the pupils but pinheads.
As I slowed he slowed.
He glanced sidelong to avoid my gaze
Then turned and retraced his steps
Out of the parking lot with its tall sodium security lamps.
Intelligent devil, saw I lacked a doggie bag
And let me pass.

Killers are everywhere, but we go out,
Drive around, walk from parking lots,
Hear the bull snuff in its stall.
May we make it to bedtime unmurdered.
Carpe diem, if you wish.
Carpe diem, little fish
Of air.
If the hummingbird stops drinking it drops dead.
There is absolutely no hesitation for decisions.
Emily Dickinson got a lot out of hummingbirds.
Maybe more than is in them.
Most rivers start as snow.
Snow is caused by the sun.
Earth is round,
But down they run.
To see anything absolutely requires madness.
Art is sunglasses.
When it gets dark
People watch TV or go to a movie or get drunk.
Some people read a book.
Some women dont shave their legs that day.
Then you sleep.
People bring you bowling balls, and say,
If you will just slice them with this kitchen knife . . .
Then you wake up.
This, of all days.

If you are death-haunted
Never drink beer, my
Dear, or you might drown
In your unshed tears.
I take my tone
From Mother Goose,
Who was a sot, and look
What it got her: shoes
Full of children, talking
Foxes, crooked men,
Fornicating spoons and dishes,
Most of chaos, compulsively
Rhyming. Everything
Had so much meaning
Naturally she was death-haunted.
All she wanted was to
Stop dreaming, but that being
An empty wish, she kept on drinking.
At least it made her woes delicious.
When the beer cans reached her ceiling
They started breeding, of course.
More chaos, more meaning.
She was as fecund as fear
And beer was her semen. So
If you are death-haunted too,
Dont drink beer, dear, or like
Mother Goose you might forget
How to cry out "Enough!", go berserk,
Sleep with your sons as soon as theyre born
And slip down and break your hip in the afterbirth.

I cut my hair.
I wear sunglasses.
I carry a platinum card.
I imitate a cowboy.
I make it my business
To bear witness
To the honeysuckle's
Accuracy and excess.
I will not let another
Pull out my stamen
And laugh at the golden
Drop on the hair.
And then he saw
A wave of alcohol
Wash over the rodeo oval.
And did not sleep
One whole night
The rest of his life.
Gradually the brave
Prince was minced
By purple swordwork
For his arrogance.
Fell from his armchair
Like dogfood,
Kuh- shlop.
Relieved of his rodeo buckle.
Lowered into the honeysuckle.

A crust of ice covers the battery.
I scrape the contacts
Until theyre bright,
Retighten the bolts on the cables
And turn the key. But it's no go.
This is a real death.
Im high up the mountain,
And everyone else has already left,
And it looks like snow.
After about thirty minutes a woman passes
In a Volvo with skis on the roof.
I wave my arms. She drives right by.
Just what I'd advise my wife to do.
It's getting dark.
Eventually a hippie in a VW stops
To give me a jump.
To him it's all theatre. He is totally stoned.
We join batteries. My car starts
And I head for the coast, all downhill
Through huge slow flakes of snow.

§ *CRAWLING THROUGH THE GRASS*
  EATING GLOWWORMS

And gaunt goateed D.H. Lawrence comes walking
From the beige and red crayon portrait on a book.
He who was the best poet who was mainly a novelist I know of.
And he stands slightly hunched over

Against the night sky almost the color he is,
Mumbling about blood-words.
His ghost risen from the ink on the page.
He can do this over and over.

He can come to me when I am in a state of mind
Requiring a glow like ultra-violet,
Or whatever is the psychological equivalent.
As he simultaneously exaggerates and pays attention.
As he plunges with no regard for his vanity

Into the black forest of his mother.

I walk 5th Ave
Seeking angels
In their pure being.
But there are so many people.
All seem like extras.
So I come home, sad
And out of Anne's hair
"Go find what makes you happy,"
She'd said. So I went
Looking for angels.
I found only one. In the elevator.
Her profile was alabaster.
Her hair was gold, then gone
Three floors above me.
My cigar smoke in the corner of my eye just scared me.
I thought it was someone coming
Toward me.

VIRGIL WILL SAY:
Think of me as your usher.
These tiny trees
Under the sidewalk grate
In front of the Museum of Modern Art
That get just enough sun
To grow only so high
Then die
Are really a dark wood
And a way to non-literal life.
Autobiography is fine,
But this is more like the bible,
Woes and wishes of humans in words.
Havent you always lived
The reclusive life
Of one who is saving himself
For the transformation of commonplace things
Into image? Then
Give me your hand.
I know you're no Christian.
Neither was I.
Pretend.
The untravelled say,
Where there's smoke, there's fire.
But not here.
Wife cannot save you.
Child cannot save you,
Savior cannot save you.
It's like when you fall asleep
And keep thinking,
Why am I back in this gradeschool? Which locker is
My locker?
You see that tall blond woman
With the holster of Evian water?
She is the flesh.
Come with me
And I'll make you red
Like the words of Jesus.
Many versions, lies of copyists, mystical literalists,
We will laugh at all that.

III   RESURRECTION

In the coffee house
The girl in the black do-rag
With the milk green stone on her forehead
Takes out her violin
And plays it, poorly.
The boy in the round glasses goes to the toilet.
We are starving in high seas.
The back of the mirror is black.
I take these liberties literally.
We are eating sardines in the Negev.
The bedouins wear Ray Bans
And serve instant coffee.
They showed me the stone
Mary's breast milk made white.
Well, it *was* white.

§   *GNAT*

I blew a gnat from the page of my book
And now I cant look
At my black pillow
For fear I will see it twisted and silver.

§ *SONG*

Ginko tree sex-enhancer
From china where
Ravines shed black mists
Nightly in daylight
Widows wed long hair in
Grass huts and hermits
Emit scrolls on loneliness and its powers.
Mushrooms, sudden, soft.
Tree sways as one ink
Brushstroke in brain.
Vine-flowers quicken
Like wakened chihuahuas.
He shaves, she shaves.
Ginko tree leafmush cures
Impotence. Good
For making woman think
He loves me.
Go, go on
Studying the little shadow
Where suave candleflame hovers
Half off wax wick,
My icon of clarity.
Though no one can
Follow this, follow.
Look long into chinese ink painting of
Black crags and mist and tiny fisherman in hat.
A specific place has an emotional quality.
To know that.
Brown Prado; silver MOMA; white National Athens.
Black fumi fishermen
To jagged crags dont matter.
All this is written
By the hatchling in the egg
Living on its
Own egg white, which is
Clear. All month though
Sun shines on tops
Of clouds below
Them it is a shadowless

Now. Now, now, dont
Cry. But there is a
Book in my eye.
It hurts, the book.
I bend over and shake
My head at the sink.
The sink says it has
No powers. I pluck at it
With a toothpick. But it
Breaks and itself sticks.
Now I am wet with
Both spirit and matter.
I give up watching protestants on TV.
I begin to watch the black clothed catholics.
So many chances to drive
Your car someplace overwhelms
You. So my rhythm is my rhythm like
I drive that way and one
Can see me coming if I get off this porch.
Something interior none can see
Is coming rhythmically toward me.
And in my transitions also they know me.
Experience, experience is what
You put the white noise between to mark your spot.
There can be a huge rhythm like war
Or you can be born during one.
You can inherit a self, or be forced
To ape family. Then you grow up
And have a face, a pace by which you are known.
But you are stopped, overwhelmed
By the chances, the choices, to be more.
Even though that seems like an ending, go on.
So long as we live, none.
The watermelon colored
Petals of the crape myrtle
Flutter to earth. I think
Two mockingbirds were mating
In it. Everything around me
Is tumescent.

But who knows
Maybe the petals
Dropped to death
And I happened
To be looking
At excess.
The Grand Canyon
As a great slaughter.
The Himalayas
As the difficult births
Of our daughters.
Looking at it that way.
The sea trench so deep
Things' eyes are lightbulbs.
Her silhouette
Through her long
Dress. I happened to be looking
At excess.
And the deepsea animal jellies are connected
By black stickbridges of self.
In nightclubs the sexes
Lean forward to touch their waving antennas.
Their thrilled roachmouths keep each other immaculate.
Their words turn matter
Into flashfloods of transparent granite.
Carry a newspaper to dinner.
Sit under an overhead light
And read. Eat the hot fudge.
Personify the napkin's whiteness.
Objects possessing perfection
Hate each other's angelic expressions.
The mucilage slug
Protests
The always
Dry ant.
Sing of Heaven.
Sing of Nothing.
A little rhyme is gladness,
A lot is madness.

This has been choral.
The tone is not gone.
To the human
Yearning and contact
Are human all through the song.

§ *GO FEED THE SWANS*

Go feed the swans.
Take them pears.
Throw out the gold
And watch their despair.
On the black mirror they float,
Fictions in their structure.
The swans, the red coals.
The lagoon's black mirror's mercury
Slides off. They are
Their own ghosts.

§ DESIRE GROWS

Desire grows. Desire for the orange,
The carnation. D.H. Lawrence's
Sulphurous glow on the horizon
Approaches. The club sodas taste better.
Soon he might be able to write letters.
Childhood is not false again.
He who shot the cardinal in the honeysuckle
And tied its talons around his neck
And woke up covered with ants.
Each poem mocks Death.
Which wants to make you not exist
And as though you had never existed.
That he might be more than unrecorded fire
Desire grows. That he might have his mind back.

§ FIRST WEDDING

I go to the First Wedding, and there are many guests;
Among them the potter whose glazes are legend;
And the great painter, the unknown, painter of turkeys
And chaos; and the great doctor and ethicist; and the barefoot
Bride with tattooed toes like red lace of India;
And the silent orange and grey sunset; and the great
Ink pen (this one) recording the passages on paper in words
Of the tablecloths with real leaves glued to them;
Short History Of Hashish In Marin;
And the great Priestess who joins the bride and the groom,
With her candles, and her bells, and her humorless authority
(For the great ink pen rolls its eyes at the Priestess);
And the great black spinach, the great crust; and the jewish glass
Crushed in the silk bag by the groom; and the bestman in a tuxedo
Juggling three red bags; and the el greco hotel at the gaunt hour
When the purple clouds merge with their background; and the Bay
Glitters no more; and the great First Wedding threatens again
Loneliness with permanent death.

§ I SEE AN ANT

I see an ant
Carrying a termite wing
Over the steel street nameplate
CHESTNUT. In front of the oxblood thorax jiggles
The little isinglass petal
Which has its own amber shadow.
One hundred and four years of wheels
Crossing the steel
Have rubbed its cross-hatchings smooth.
It would take a lot of ants to do such a thing.
Fewer if each carried a termite wing.

§ *THE ISLANDERS*

I step behind them
On the escalator, into the wake
Of the odor of Islanders.
They are four females
And smell like fruitdrops,
The candy of war, hair
Slicked up stiff as black
Ice, plaid skirts of their school,
Looking at themselves
In the stainless steel
Of the escalator above them.
Because I am white, with a white beard,
They think me no man to fear.
And I can stand very near
Their black plaid.

Opening, the banana flower, purifies
The stainless steel range, bruise
Colored petals curling
To show the embryo bananas,
Puts through the acid
And peels steel to its boiling
Point, the objective and scentless
Banana flower, a stem
In the jelly jar magnified,
Baby bananas green as
Grass blades, bends its mass,
Violet, fruits and purifies
All that is objective around it.

Hail to Charles
Bukowski, hymnist
Of booze and pudenda, poetry's
Breughel, who also
Wrote prose (which Ive never
Read so cant praise it). Hail
To plain talk
Elevated to film noir, to
Confession and autobiography
And intelligent Chaucerian
Vulgarity, in which East of Eden
Is Los Angeles and bums
Drive BMWs and
Shakespeare smokes Camels
In bars with iron doors.
Hail to the colloquial
Grace of his timing, to his
Mixture of Fact and Vision,
To the way his poems all
Sound alike but are not, like Bach.
Shame on the fact
That the nerds of American poesy
Ignored him while the Intellectuals
Of Europe held him aloft. Hail
To him as the best streetpoet since Whitman,
And God save us all
From his imitators.

Hail to Louis Zukofsky, poetry's
Mondrian, who disapproved
Of the poem as heroic act,
Who wore a tweed suit and a tie every day
And "would not go out into his own
Backyard unshaved."
Master craftsman and maker
Of music light as pine
Needles brushing or dense as the mule's
Foot, obsessive rewriter
And distruster of religious epiphanies,
We praise you, we praise
Your mathematical spiderwebs
Of steel hairs, your harps,
Your willingness to carry self-
Discipline to the point of
The heroic excess you scorned,
Your lyrics, your long
Objective nose and round eyeglasses, we
Praise your poems
That go on and on
Like history when viewed
From the present. Hail to Zukofsky!
At least to the Zukofsky who wrote Zukofsky's songs!

§ THE SALESGIRLS IN THE WESTERN STORE

What order of beauty are they,
These cowgirls whose buckles
Are silver saucers,
Who ring up your sale with one arm
While with the other nursing
A baby with more hair than a man?
And they are not dumb.
They have put in their places violent men.
Round-armed, helpful, sweet, foul-mouthed,
Kind on the phone, sarcastic when they hang up,
Green eyes small and close together,
Castrators of horses, too large for small jeans,
Difficult to intimidate, used to being
Cheated on, and generally cheating. What
Order of beauty are they, these cowgirls?
Now that the orders of Helen and Hecate are taken . . .

§ *THE POWER OF PRAYER*

When the Queen of the Persians
Came to pour milk
On her husband's grave
To honor the dead
Recently slaughtered
In shallow water
I was stunned.
Envisioning that milk
Working its way
To the black underworld
Where they believed
Dead souls
Lay to drink
Made me believe,
The words.

§ IN K-MART

Latin in the black fields.
Personas of the cow bones.
Shaving the log for kindling.
The blueblack wetness of another's feelings.
In the brain, even its stem.
Following the fragments
Until the illusion of narrative
Is experienced as the facecards in solitaire.
Until Latin is spoken also in the pickups.
In K-Mart where the cathedral's vividness
Is duplicated. Where you can buy big snips
To snip your chains. And everyone
Walks around noisily free,
Place most loathed by ghosts.

Under an awning of water,
The meeting of bellboy
And woman in red silk and diamonds.
She hands him the keys to her car.
There is a slight jingling of metal.
She enters the black oval of the restaurant
And the scene closes behind her,
Bereft of its most violent color. Memory
Supplies the velvet and nails
To construct the stage
On which we witness the interactions
Of people who have never met
But there. Even the dead laugh
At barbeques and discuss the skinny green dragonfly.
It selects, it praises, it sifts
The unendurable pains
And sweetens the rest with gold lamplight
So that even the child's deathbed
Seems only its radiant necessities.
Over our lives this transparent awning
Arches and crests.
And we walk from it. Drenched, drowned, dead,
But not wet!

§ CLOTH ROSES IN THE DRAWER UNDER THE PLACEMATS

Under the black placemats
In the kitchen drawer, soft
As an animal, as rodents,
I uncover your hump,
And there are the cloth roses,
Dry roses,
Beyond fakeness, neither dead nor alive.
Open the dictionary to any word:
None is fake.

The specter ogled the spring bubbling up in the clover.
No animal comes from its burrow in sorrow.
Here is the host of the larvae
Born in the blood of the lamb.
Long trembles the gong.
Motes in the cathedral's stained glass sunbeam
Burst like sperm
From the teenager touched by the hand
With the fingernails.
I will get used to pain says the invalid,
I will be like a pearl necklace
Broken and loose in a drawer.
Until I have summed up my values and compared them to death.
Until the sere stone is covered
With the spring that bubbles from clover
And runs from one sand grain to another
Like genes between lovers.

§ CAN YOU SAY

Can you say you have been improved
By the bloody Iliad, Stan.
By the Gregorian Chants. When you hear
Those baritones in the echoing stone
Are you permanently increased. Can you say
By Raphael's The Transfiguration you have been raised.
I can say these things changed the paths of my brain
Cells, shaped me, made me
The poor thing I am.

Poor gorged
Clay thing,
Barely able
To pull his chair
Up to the Last
Supper table.
I love close-harmony singing.
It's like the reassuring smell of dry cleaning.
But I digress.

Assume that you are destroyed by something,
But dont know it. And go on living as if
Your glaze were smooth, and not crazed.
Until one extra feather is laid
Upon you and you break into pieces,
Each piece with legs.

My tale is done
Like the sun
Which will return.

§ I HAVE COME

I have come from
The air drenched
With greenness
To the treeless beauty
Of the ocean.

Those who would know the emotional quality
Cannot ignore Pound's ear, his timing. And I left
My son in the dorm room. Kissed his whiskered
Babyskin cheek, and blew him another. As he
Walked off with two girls named Elizabeth.
Or ignore his raptor's eye, or forgive him
His monomanias, and the light of his
Mind like the light on wavelets that cannot
Cohere or reach shore. This is what Ezra
Pound means to me on the day after I leave
My son at Brown University and sit in this
Room in New York wondering what to do next.
Fixed in one place like the wavelets that
Imitate livingness. Is this modern enough?
Anne, you hedge-full-of-lightning-bugs,
When I close my eyes I can see you. The sparkling
Behind eyelids, who is it? Now
She is I, the ordinal, whipping the horses
To a lather as I tremble in the haycart
Behind her that tips on two wheels at the
Precipice. In dreams she lashes the horses. And
Forever the corn smells of sun as I walk into it
To urinate. What happened in time
Stays in time. Now even our images are entangled.
Root out the horses, they have
Grown tendrils from their steel shoes and
Though my books are in no bookstores,
Root out the horses. This is the Second Day.
There stand the carriage horses. They tread
Their golden droppings. Some people pass
Holding maps to their noses. That horse
Is the color of rust in sun. They could
Not pull fireplaces, or orange coals and iron.
That would take Homer, Winslow. He's at the
Met now. Let's go over. Here we are. This
Is dangerous. In the painting of the fox in the snow
Are the world's best crows. There is
Green in their blackness. Then there's the
Watercolor of the leaves and the oranges.
And the one of the fogbank creeping

To strand the rowboat from the mothership. Faux forces
Thrash the black water to foam. But Im
Disappointed. He is not our Vermeer. I bet
Hopper liked him. Now let's go buy
Some neat clothes. Of course we dont Need
Them. But the salesgirl wears flesh
Skipants, butchlength blond hair, and eyes
Crystalized in Antarctica. Save me! In
Homer's green net of death I struggle like
A wig in a washing machine. And then the
Moment is over. And only her profile in the
Mirror as she hands my credit card back to me.
Rapunzel, reach down your little hands, too.
It is troubling to me that our greatest songster
Was crazy. This, the transitional century.
None other such swift change. And
The gleaming at the box edge as the lid
Is lifted. Angels, monsters, in coitus. The box
Hot as a lightbulb. From in it, labor-pain screams
Muffled by mother of pearl. To
Know the emotional quality, lest grief
Break the egg of the skull. Irrational,
The songster's transitions, but also like
Those of the waves. Oh, really? Now night
Has fully fallen on New York. The streetlamps
Shiver in Queens over the invisible East River.
Chris in Providence. Anne in Chicago. And
My future shorter now, though the babics
In strollers look the same age as ever. Night is
Earth's shadow on itself. One of Winslow's
Crows drinks from a downspout in New Orleans,
Whether witnessed or not. In the broken glass
Shade of a streetlamp in Central Park a bird
Builds her nest, the lightbulb for warmth.
Sparrows fall as often as leaves and God is
Distracted to madness. Only the nazis kept excellent
Records. Behold! They are the golfers in lightning.
Three days passed. Jesus rose on a seashell,
Hand shielding vulva, at last, masculine.
The only religion to start with a murder,

Said Anne. I dont get it. The babe in the stroller,
Its eyes liquid nickels. Forgive it? Two fawns
Stiffen at streamside. Spots of sun
In their fur. They have come down to drink
From the stream I am squatting in. The doe
Mother, also, rigid. Moment of wholeness.
A twitch, and they crash off through the sticks
And the hair of my flesh stood up (Job 4:15).
The emotional quality of the moment is
The religious experience of the atheist. This
Is Day Three. Ezra Pound makes me sit
Under the gold painted equestrian statue
At Central Park South and 5th.
Where some kind of needle has its way with a thimble.
Next to me sits a smooth man. Obsessed with the
Physical. Im 40. Im 6 one. 180.
Im not little but Im not big. This big
Black guy. 250. He jumps me. I fended
Him off. The cops come. Five years I had
Stayed in the house. I hadnt gone out. I
Dont know why. But this got me out. I said
Im gonna live. So the next night I went to
A bar. An Irish bar. My kind. Im talking
To this female. Her boyfriend is sitting
At the other end of the bar. For twenty minutes
We talk. I didnt know. Then he yells Hey
That's my woman youre with. And I say,
I want no trouble with you, Im not fighting
No whiteman. And he says, Why NOT?
When I reach to shake his hand he smiles and says
No, man. Germs. So we touch fistknuckles and I cross
The street and head up 5th to the Museum of
Modern Art show, Picasso and Portraiture.
When the rowboat is swamped, when the lilies
In it are level with the water, I see the
Glass ball paperweight of snowflakes in oil
Of the moment, the rose window in the cool
Cathedral, and for our delectation. I enter
The museum, tense that the tentacles of the
Masters might brush me, that the suckers

Crowning granite. Carriage drivers in T-shirts
And tophats, reading the newspapers. Each
Moment, blossoming. Woman in pink silk
Pants and bullethole caste mark. Beyond all
Opinion, blossoming. And from the depths
The de-winged humans, whom the iguanas cant
Carry: cherryblack, olive, glistening, sitting
On the benches, eating. Of the millions of acts
In a moment, most of them kindnesses.
Out of the anonymity and loneliness of liberty,
Kindnesses. Comes the most difficult hour.
A text is demanded.
Some find surrender impossible. Some sleep.
Fourth Day. Nothing. Fifth Day.
Soon they discovered the grass was greener
Where the shit fell. But
I weary of climbing this ladder into the peach
Colored clouds for fear that if I do not
I will wear the S&M hood of the wasted life.
A James Ensor painting is making me say this.
Every day, every day, Leisure is Evil
And Fun the golfpro of Death.
I would walk out into the
Trees of the Park were my ankles not aching
So much. This punishment for climbing the hours.
Softly, a streetperson, a mixture
Of the Grim Reaper and Santa, approacheth.
Freaks out even the other streetpeople.
And at 57th and 6th a woman dressed only
In a ripped plastic garbage bag raps her
Cup on the sidewalk. I swear, aware of her
Part in the play. And nearby in Army Square
A whitewoman in khaki and orange plaid,
Expertly accessorized, cries out You will
NOT take money from my account, Thank you!
You will NOT, do you hear me? Stands, smooths her
Hair, juts forth a steel chin, and vanishes.
I am reporting as I was ordered.
Perhaps Woolworths has plain white china.
Paranoia is the logical madness. I, too,

Walk the streets arguing things out. They
Can see my lips moving. I am constantly
Eating a lifesaver so maybe theyll think
He is eating a lifesaver. Well, if you dont
Say it out loud it's not true. Thinking, alone,
Wont do. Thinking alone wont do. That's why
We each need privacy. So we can talk. If you
Dont get out more often, Im telling you,
The gods will think you dont care. My ankles
Are killing me, OK? I look up. I see
In the mirror a Fujifilm blimp. If I sleep well
And dream of vengeance, I wake up exhausted.
Of course, there is sex; and those moments
When the landscape looks handmade; and a
Painting of apples resembles three severed
Heads from the bible; and the limousines
Are lined up in front of The Plaza sniffing
Each other. These can be milked. And there are
Measures of time. For example, how long
Does it take a manhole cover to be
Worn a smooth silver by tires? That is not
Without intelligence. Then there are those who say
Being, not doing, is the true path. Well, being
Makes me very nervous, and I would rather
Be a lapdog on Madison than a lotus, than a
Deep-breathing lotus. I told the waitress I wanted
My eggs poached hard. They were runny. But
Her eyes were so green and her hand so hairless.
Black jeans. Gold gravy. Offspring of foam.
I got what I wanted. Said my two year old son
On observing his erection as I changed his diaper
My penis is tall! I will walk to the Met again,
Hobbled, cursing the details. Wanting, as always,
Only to have my skin, like a nightgown,
Pulled off me. Wanting the next step
After nakedness. The biological equivalent of
El Greco's "View Of Toledo." But it does
Not happen. Quite the opposite. The quartz
In the watch is inaudible. The church
Until recently punished masturbation by broiling,

85

And the hole midway down the puritan nightgown
Closed like a crocodile's nostril,
While even the bananas jerked off. Night
Of the Fifth Day. Morning of the Sixth. Note:
The Theory Of Dissipative Structures suggests
That in an open system far-from-equilibrium
Complex patterns can arise from simple ingredients
Provided that energy is continually pumped in
And waste entropy is removed. Some scientists
See this as an explanation for the origin
And evolution of life in which a flow of
Energy from the sun is dissipated as it powers
The creation of complexity. I am having a
Fine time. I have to force myself but each
Morning I go get a café americano which I
Drink while reading the NY Times on a bench
At 6th and Central Park South. The stench of the
Horse manure I find rather pleasant, like
State Fairs and Pastoral Painting, though
Some people passing hold the collars of their
Shirts to their faces and pick up their step.
When the sun appears from behind the building
That shades me the heat of its light hits me
Suddenly, knifelike, rather than gradually
As one might assume given the slowness
Of shadows. It's all or nothing, you know.
My mood is anxious and fragile. It used to be
I couldnt imagine being bored or depressed,
All things being miracles. I seem to be destined
To suffer everything I once couldnt imagine.
Perhaps suffer is too strong a word. But you know
Me. I am writing a long poem which I hope
Deals with the structure of experience. It's
Some kind of excessivist theory about the
Psychological states you can be in over a given
Period and still maintain dynamic balance
In a system that otherwise seems about to resolve
Into equilibrium, which is death. Today
I discovered the paintings of Paula Rego and she
Knows what I mean. I stopped at the carousel

In the Park and while I was there I was happy.
The guy who was running it eventually started
To stare at me as though I were some kind
Of pedophile, so I left. Cupid was chasing chasing
A rabbit rabbit with his brown bow and arrow.
One horse had a backward lion skin for a saddle
And another had its red tongue hanging out
Almost like in life. Then I went on to
The big sculpture of Alice In Wonderland.
Alice and the Creatures are bronze rubbed
Bright by the children who've climbed them. In
The ground surrounding the sculpture are
Bronze plaques with quotes from the book.
I read one about a little boy who was spanked
For sneezing that disturbed me so much I
Walked off. I think it had something to do
With my dream last night in which I was
Naked from the waist down and this fully
Dressed woman reached under my t-shirt
And threatened to squeeze my balls. I was
Paralyzed and humiliated and paralyzed. I
Woke up and said to myself It's only
A dream. But was it? But I do not know. Actually
Things are going fine. I look forward to working
On the poem each day. I am on the 29th page and I do
Not read what I have previously written any more than
I go through all my past life before leaving the
I just struck out the last 29 words. I shouldnt
Mention the poem. But the people, the people
Seem most estranged of all things. Love,
Your husband. P.S. Will I tell you that dream
On the phone? The Seventh Day. I pick up the string
In the cream of the late afternoon. In each
Doorway of Times Square stands a minotaur. I pull
On the string. One suit says to another Go
To Atlantic City. Take three or four hundred
Dollars. You lose it. OK. Dont take scared money.
My paintings will see the dawn sun before I do.
Can fire melt them down any further, that have
Been through the furnace of brain? When the hive

Is on fire do the worker bees
Crackle and writhe at the door
To save the queenbee, or flee? Once the image is in it,
It's in it. Nor will oil paint evaporate from
The forehead, nor bullshit not show up in the verse.
The fake Rolexes in the briefcases are golder
Than real Rolexes are, and in the Africans
Selling them no drop of slavery, no cream.
The penis can double in size. The iron bridge
Swells in the heat. I yank on the string.
The bull bursts into the cruelly round ring.
Things change. Splice them. First overwrite, then splice.
In magical thinking if you mention death you will die.
In logical thinking if you dont mention death etc.
And the soul floats between like a jellyfish
Blown on the wind. Is death masculine?
After rigor mortis again comes softness.
Death with a scythe is a plague image.
Death as a sniper, now that, said Winslow Homer,
Is the closest thing in war to sheer murder.
If the hours pass unused I feel terror. Death's
Hand under (long red fingernails) the hem of my t-shirt.
End all long poems with a monkey.
I saw in the silence a demon
Whittling a length of aluminum, where the collie
Ran the wire fence, day and night barking,
And one day died, and his owner came
With a pitchfork and stuck it in him
And carried him off over his shoulder.
Any questions? One.
Was Freud right that the soul is a narrative?
I just read palms, son, the palms of Miami. Jesus
Cracketh no jokes. As surely as the Prado is brown
I will get this song down in
Words. On the back of the t-shirt worn by the black man
Pushing the cart out of which was coming
A quavering tenor was printed
The Voice You Hear Singing Is Me.
He *seemed* to be headed toward Heaven.
I stare down into the empty

Washing machine, so clean,
Its paddles as smooth as a photo.
This, also, sits at the right hand of God.
Throne of the Senses. A monkey can figure out
A slide-bolt easily so dont use one of those
On its cage, nor, if you do, cry out
When you come home to find it escaped
And on the refrigerator eating handful by handful
Your chocolate cake. You are Adam
To it. So it screams, and leaps into your arms
And clings, like a human, being. The gods
Are the slaves of our prayers, poor babies. And
Only the sun cannot walk in the cool of the day.

A NOTE ON THE TYPE

The text of this book was set in Sabon, a typeface designed by Jan Tschichold (1902–1974), the well-known German typographer. Because it was designed in Frankfurt, Sabon was named for the famous Frankfurt type founder Jacques Sabon, who died in 1850 while manager of the Egenolff foundry.

Based loosely on the original designs of Claude Garamond (c. 1480–1561), Sabon is unique in that it was explicitly designed for hot-metal composition on both the Monotype and Linotype machines as well as for film composition.

Composition by NK Graphics, Keene, New Hampshire
Printed at The Stinehour Press, Lunenburg, Vermont
Bound by Quebecor Printing, Brattleboro, Vermont
Designed by Harry Ford